Ditch-tender

Ditch-tender

Poems by

Julia B. Levine

UNIVERSITY OF TAMPA PRESS · TAMPA, FLORIDA

Cover art: "Opera Singer with Bike" by Alexandra Rozenman from the collection of Rebecca Barns, Providence, R.I., reproduced by permission of the artist. www.alexandrarozenman.com

Manufactured in the United States of America
Printed on acid-free paper ∞
First Edition

The University of Tampa Press
401 West Kennedy Boulevard
Tampa, FL 33606

ISBN 978-1-59732-037-5 (hbk) • ISBN 1-59732-038-2 (pbk)

Browse & order online at
http://utpress.ut.edu

Library of Congress Cataloging-in-Publication Data

Levine, Julia B.
  Ditch-tender : poems / by Julia B. Levine. -- 1st ed.
    p. cm.
  ISBN 978-1-59732-037-5 (acid-free paper) -- ISBN 978-1-59732-038-2 (pbk. : acid-free paper)
  I. Title.
  PS3562.E89765D58 2007
  811'.54--dc22   2007031975

Contents 🦋

I.

II.

III.

for my father, Mark C. Levine

Water says: …
Wherever you put me, I'll be in my home.
I am awfully smart. Lead me out of my springs,
lead me from my rivers, but I came from the ocean
and I shall go back into the ocean.
You can dig a ditch and put me in it, but I go only so far
and I am out of sight. I am awfully smart.
When I am out of sight I am on my way home.

–Wintun Indian woman
as told to Demetrocopolou, 1935

I.

After the Flood

Strange, how beautiful torment has made this cove:

an estuary hurtling down hills, blasting roads and bridges,
crushing a path through the willows.

The dock, unhinged, bobs out at sea.

How perfect it seems:
landscape no longer a fact, but a being

drowning in the milky silt
the wind lifts and swirls,

a child stumbling out in coat and boots,
asking, *What have I forgotten?*

Now a heron starts his wings,
glint like a flock of swallows
grazing the scrabbled wash and bay.

And the molten crust that anchors a body, a bed,
shaken loose and battered

into a bewilderment

the girl sifts through. Kneeling deep inside the windfall
of white shells, dark pools,

can you see how devoted she is

to learning this momentary world
as disturbance,

as the next lost place?

Proof, As Near As I Can Tell

Last of the fog burning back,
she looks out my office window, and tells me

there was an experiment in her dream last night:

an infant that needed to be studied,
and so she unswaddled it, rubbed the clitoris.

Watched the tiny face

register pleasure and distress
at once. *At the same time*, she says, and cries.

Now is the time to say something small
to save her life.

And not the things I've already said.

Like, *What changes slowly, perfectly, is invisible.*
Or, *Imagine yourself before the small desks of school.*

No, today I want to tell her, *Memory drags the river*
of all that is desperate to escape.

Find the openings where the gone world
empties the present. Go deeper in.

But I don't.
Instead, a train whistles. My rocker groans.

Instead, I lay a kleenex across her knees.

Down below, someone is taking tickets
and someone is boarding the train. *I'm bloated with loneliness*

she says. *I'm going to die without ever having been loved
in someone else's hands.*

Over the stationary store, the train station, the barbershop,
swallows circle the city

before sifting down. *Please, look at me,*
I say. *I want you to know I'm here.*

And then she does, speaking so softly
I have to kneel before the couch

to hear her say, *Strange, how scared I am—*

and it's true, her hands are trembling, the mortal house
convulsed and shaken

just to tell me
that she knows the experiment is about turning away.

How it can kill you. How she woke

this morning from the dream
knowing she didn't want to die. Not from that. Not yet.

Let us empty this room of facts

while children fly through the indoor pool, squealing,
wingbuds of their missing arms and legs,

a threshold
where weight slides most easily into water.

The stump is innocent.

The three-legged boy, fluid as a seal.

I take a shower listening to two girls
in the stalls beside mine, singing,

picturing the city out those windows:
rain arguing bitterly with the bay,
taxis ferrying all the joined and perfect couples.

What does it mean to say something is missing?

One of the girls holds her towel with her teeth,
her arm ending like a sausage, taut and handless.

Admit it.

It's not the loneliness
that makes you stare.

It's the fear
you might never embody the damage
of your life

as they do—
wholly, exactly as it is.

Bat Ray

I wanted to touch it, just once, netted and spilled,
a wild darkness knocking against the white hush of sky.

I wanted to touch the determined light of it,
the animal deftness that cannot be held

but that fights to stay alive
and turns from its own mother

if it has to, if she can't stop herself
from telling stories and laughing about it:

You were a baby and mad as hell
that we were leaving, so your father went in

and slapped you quiet for the sitter.
And the ray giving a little cry

when I grab the rubbery wetness
to throw it back in, its teeth

razoring a red arc around my hand.
Like climbing through, just once, just behind it,

that's where I wanted to touch the glint of it—
the first cause, that self-created being

to which every chain of causes must ultimately go back—
that's where I thought I'd find the light

of those six months before my father started in—
that place where light begins,

hatches from its green carapace,
Tomales Bay parting as the ray slips back in

and disappears,
and how the cove comes together again,

so easily, so gracefully.
It has that power—water, light—

to forget the disturbance, the damage,
so completely, you have to wonder,

was it there at all?

Driving West on 37, Listening to the Sonic Memorial

Why stop ever, days of rain
lifting rust from winter's sedge,

a taste of unfinished ruin
shuttled and looming

in the storm of swallows
giving back the massive river,

the voice on my radio
unsealing the beyond,

binding it back again.
Jules, this is David. I am on a plane

that's been taken hostage,
and it doesn't look good,

a flock of swallows flying now
across the marsh, folding the silver edges

over and over, the great barriers
dissolving up that high

where David whispers, *Jules,*
I want you to know. I loved you absolutely.

Finally, I think, the smallness
of believing in one body

is all that ever can be undone.
How I hear David's voice

and want him to live; want Jules
to beg him, *Please, come back,*

but of course she isn't home,
the tiny tape on her counter

turning round his ghost,
a strange whir unloosed and soaring.

As if the instinct to return
were embedded in us too,

a magnetic field poured and snowing
through the body's static

into air, the way David does now,
my own face changing shape

to think of how he is hurled into it—

like fledglings pushed from cliffs,
like the ones at the tower's edge

feeling the floor begin to crumble—
how finally, at the edge of all we know,

they are taking someone's hand,
they are throwing two bodies

against one sky, one wing

Golden Gate

For the lonely, the bridge is a seam between two skies.
And sky, the lowest register of sleep.

Once a colleague of mine locked her baby in a room
and drove two hours out to this bridge to die.

And driving through these fields of mustard,
not even a glimpse of two bulls fighting in the hills

could keep my friend from climbing the guardrail,
skirt hiked up.

Now my daughter opens her mouth to the radio's song,
face turned toward the window,

and I see I was mistaken:
I've been speaking to my younger self all along,

swaying on the bridge up there, a handful of pills
sleek as bullets cupped against her lips.

Tell me, what is loneliness,
if not the strain of standing at the edge of all you know?

Look, my daughter says suddenly,
pointing to the ocean's watery nothing.

Which is beautiful and blue and carnal. For the sea,
everything that matters is the sky

as it is interrupted by a bridge: thinnest line
that can hold two worlds together

without becoming one.

Gristled Angels

i.

They were lovely once, untouched.
But at midnight in the Tenderloin, they are laying out
the rags and wrappers and half-finished sodas—
they are displaying lamps, pamphlets,
even a prosthetic leg
that the youngest crack-head touches,
flicking her hair back in a gesture
left from middle school, and who knows,
stoned as she is, whether the plastic foot
looks like a twisted wand
or a nostalgic galaxy of sinew,

or why the doper lunges at her
with a knife, until running,
blood everywhere, she thinks,
It tastes like salt, it tastes like home.

ii.

This week, in my office, the boy
the social worker brings,
arrives in a rising tide of terror,
until it seems his mother crouches there,
behind my couch, clutching a razor,
while his small arms, his fierce bite,
strike and grab her hair

instead of mine, instead of me—

though I kneel over him,
glazed with sweat and spit,
holding on.

And when the boy
finally slips back into his body,
I touch his cheek.

He looks up.
Asks, *Is it true?*
Can you really break your heart?

iii.

Swept down, and slowly
in the dark, in silence,
there is a deep soreness, an accidental opening,
where I've let hope too far in,

while around the bay,
water fingers the elliptical shores
rimmed in scotch broom.
Here one could wake.

Or go on drifting
in a small craft
as the weather suddenly turns wrong
—wind blowing hard out of South—

the sea's enormous swells
fighting my scull,

the world's complicated armada of suffering
floating out of that boy's beginning—his mother
        waking, at fourteen, from a weeklong high.

Even if the gristled angels rise like buoys;

even if we have to motor through the dark water
of the otherworld,

do you see how easily a child grasps
that he is unfinished?

That the vile story has to be lanced
before he can become a pocket again
for light, for nothing
but the present—
astonishing in its plain speech, its possibility.

Bathtime at the Children's Shelter

and I'm trying to be brave, to dab his penis
with this towel, to unfold his twisted arm
and rub the inside dry.
Last week, they wanted me to say
whether it was better if a man or woman
held him down, while the doctor checked
how many times he'd been torn apart.
And sure I'm paid to live this close
to the dirt of what's been done,
but I don't know about these red scabs
exploding across the child's skin.
Or how he sits on the toilet, thin as a rail,
trembling from the cold, and speaks
as if he's fine. *Go ahead,*
he tells me cheerfully,
just let the good one help the bad,
and together we fish his crippled hand
through the pajamas his father gave to him.
Power Rangers, he says, and smiles.
Annie, I nearly said to his favorite aide.
But we don't talk
about how little is coming clean.
And though the good in me
seems a worn-out rag, I'm nodding
as he tells me his father wants him back,
and kneeling as I lift his legs, one by one,
into the pajama legs. And he's leaning, briefly,

on my shoulder, trusting me to carry,
for just a moment, the blessed
and shaming lesson
we've been asked to live.

Flyway

First consider summer ending
in the frail squall of rain

and the clamor, the louder saw of wings
that means *flocking*—

terns and coots, pelicans, a thousand cormorants
landing just outside your office door.

Consider how the fog persists.
Not the form of it, but how the edges rub and fray
the dock, the apartment building, the child's mother packing,

her mother dissolving into white.

Now the child has a fever, a sore throat.   It hurts to speak.
It hurts to know the wind will carry everything away,
                                    counting six, seven, infinity.

If despair is the distance you will not let a child cross alone,
imagine sitting close as she will let you.

Imagine convincing her suffering is not an invention,
just an error you have to help her see

as the scar between before and after.
As radiance

nearly smothered behind months of want,
a collapse of wings waiting
                    there, there . . .

Three O'Clock Patient

The race went past my office.
I'd seen them gathering there—
a parade of dads and children and college students

lining the streets strung with yellow tape.
They'd even cordoned off the parking lot,
so I wasn't surprised that she was late,

unbuttoning her raincoat, laying her umbrella
down beside the couch. *Sorry,*
she said first. And then, *I don't know,*

meaning why she'd waited inside the crowd,
craning around the corner of 3rd and C.
I don't need to tell you, she explained,

meaning that she did,
how rich a metaphor this must be—
an afternoon devoted to watching people

arrive precisely where they belong,
and just as suddenly, disappear.
Three white petals stuck to her boots

from the fruitless pear trees
blossoming up and down my block.
We could hear a radio traveling near,

then far. Yesterday, she explained,
she'd curled up on his small bed,
and there was dust across the nightlight

she couldn't bear to wipe away.
There was silence in my office then;
the kind that swells and presses hard.

Though I don't need to tell you,
meaning that I do, how hard it is
to earn good money for saying nothing

when all you've ever wanted
is to make it smaller, or less, or better.
Funny thing, she went on. *I turned my head*

at the wrong minute, and missed it all.
Meaning the bikers, the blur of speed and color.
Meaning there is nothing anyone can say

that might change the cost
of believing in forever. Even like she did.
Even for just a moment.

Eighteen Days of Fog and Rain

i.

A trapeze of seabirds
Dips across the Pacific's graveyard.

Slender flutes of white
Torpedo into the future's accident.

And who can resist stepping into the tidal madness
Of narcissus, snowbells, pale daffodils,

Believing love for one thing
Might bring another back?

Believing these starry brooms
Nosing up through the underworld,

Are the bog's ecstatic argument
With the poet I read last night, lamenting

I wish God were not inside me.

ii.

As if death were not itself a meaning,
Our children want to hear the story

Again, of the vanished that return:
The boy the mother cannot hold

Against the tsunami's suck,
Though later the father finds him

Clinging to a tree, an upturned boat.
Alive. Dead. It's not the boy who matters,

But the telling, everyone leaning forward
Into their own original scars:

Love and desolation
A constant undertow

To the exhausted breath
Of time

iii.

If we have to die to begin again;
If we must learn to let go

Of each other more easily;
Is it sadness or awe, I feel then,
Watching my youngest carry her chickens
Over the flooded pond?

And there, at the edges,
I can see my child moving deeper

Into the volatile perfume
Of flesh and rain.

Yes, say it is possible:

The silent clock of being
Shutters and opens all at once.

Say she has to touch it for herself—
The long threads of faith

We swing from—
And so she drops her flock

One by one—Yes,
Say those startled, stupid birds

Fall
Beyond such useless wings.

Easter Sunday on the American River

An old man sits on the bridge, in rain.
Below him, geese float between picnic tables.

Flooded roads, flooded park.

And there, drowning underneath these fields,
the summer our eldest was a child,

and wasn't that the lawn,
and that the spot we picnicked on?

Then, it was hot enough to fall in love
with cottonwoods sowing ghostly seeds.

Though today, only the greening canopies
fork through the gleam.

Remember her white heat of hair?

Her clouded face following the river
after a stick you threw as warning?

Now it's nearly dusk.

A white truck grumbles along the levee road
past lush hills, poppies dimming down to stars.

All night, rangers will map the rain
as it seeps into the darkest wells, the tucked-in
stones.

The man bows to the bill you hand him.

Is this all it takes to disappear?

We were so much younger once,
we didn't know.

Napa

At the restaurant, my father tells us
what the doctors said to him—*Two years at most.*

Outside, wild rye moves in the wind
No, he insists, when I ask him if he is scared.

Violet scarves of sunlight float out across the sky.
Driving home, the girls read the names of towns

we pass each time we come this way.
This is the closest we get to leaving. A dream

passing through the darkened houses, doomed yards.
The body of forgetting

just before it unbuttons a life, climbs back into history's arms.

River Road

If memory can abduct you, can return you
    to the creek behind a school, a chill light
        making atonement of the foxglove,

then once again a man spreads pictures
    of naked women on the rocks before me.
        So that driving the river road tonight,

I am lying down again, in iris, waiting
    for the holiness he promised
        two bodies together would become.

And even the dusk that denotes the world's end
    for now; even the quiet snowing darkly around a girl
        outside the church, crying into her cell phone,

recalls me once more to the detective, slowly
    turning photos, apologizing, *Sweetheart, I'm sorry,*
        but I need you to take your time.

So that I may never know exactly where I am going
    as I speed home, listening to an American general
        recently returned from war.

He sounds calm, but sad. *There were no plans,*
    he says, quietly. *No directives. I didn't know*
        who wanted our help, and who wanted us dead.

And then he falls silent. If forgetting is a blessing,
   then why is it impossible? *Begin at the beginning,*
      the radio interviewer says.

First I was a girl. And then a stranger asked to touch me.
   No, the creek was first. And iris. And foxglove.
      No, start over. First there was beauty.

Descant

Tonight, the moon broods in a house poured with light.
Gulls cry over the darkening sea, and it is hours
since the notebooks you were carrying
        shot into the streets like swallows.

Then the jeweler, still in his apron, raced out
to unpin you from the car, and holding your shattered legs
together in the gutter, barked orders for me
to slip my sweater underneath your head.

                  Poor stranger,
who knows how deep a pool
the day is, or where fate drowns
the future we can no longer have.

        Tonight, I listen to water
dream along the lips of shore.
The ramp creaks up and down the pier,
the way you must drag a heavy chain
in and out of morphine.

                Truth is,
I came here years ago with a gun and whiskey,
praying for courage. And I don't know why

I unloaded that chamber
into a black bay and watched the water
become a field of listening.

        I only know that the morning
I drove back into my life, ruined,

I was too far away from this moment
to see a woman staring out at moon
unrolling its sheets of gleam across the bay,

as if gazing into a mirror of her losses,
believing a second, more complicated melody
ripens inside the shadow's fruit,

    ready, finally,
    to live its tender song out loud.

Almost

> All night the wind wanting
to repair the abandoned elevations of sky,
the reticent chorus of stars,
> a rusted hoist
>> lifted up,
clanging down.

And then suddenly it is clear
> and unmistakably bright,
groves of fir chiming, the last glass poured,
bottles tossed,

>> heedless arias of afternoon
>> humming in the tindered brush.

>> What do we know of rain?

Now you unlock the car, warm the engine.
I shake out blankets, pack dishes,

call and call for the children to come

>>> —a singing
>> among the gulls and loons. A singing
almost swallowed
> as the children rush the shore, yelling

"Don't go! We're really here!"

What do we know of restraint?   Of anything

this enormous, and the shape it makes

    as it carries the milky fields of sky
    close enough to brush the earth,

but doesn't—

but holds them carefully
as wildflowers, as frightened stars,

        a nearly unbearable tenderness
          to come this near, this far . . .

Heaven

Just beyond the shore,
the August hills undress in gold,

swallows chirring in the sparked lagoon.
And there, nestled in the sedge,

flies ripening a fetal deer,
the scythe-curved spine, a bit of muzzle

tucked beneath the still-black hooves,
and a child, not quite seven, carrying the silence after,

her face struggling against the exploded facts.
My hand presses lightly on her arm

as I explain kindness as a wound
that ends before it hurts.

We climb the dunes.
She lies beside me on the crusted sand,

staring up at clouds, and the bluegreen light
she floats toward

is the ordinary engine of the Pacific
churning up the waves, kelp, purple vella.

A little wind stirs the sand,
leaving tiny tracks, a kind of listening

and taking note. Under the salted light,
a couple sleeps nearby,

while the sea goes on swelling and bursting open
and ripening again.

There is an hour before my child speaks,
before an enormous flock of pelicans

floats in formation overhead.
Do we call it heaven,

because instead of gravity, there are birds?
Because the down-below

has to take the dark back from her bones,
before the baby deer can fly?

We Take the Children to San Juan Capistrano

When I first wanted to be Christian, it was the melodrama
    of the candles: their sputter, faint, and flame.

        And the way time leaned so heavily against music,
a particular eternity of bells asking
        if madness could be renamed as vision

It was the astonishment of a season
                just for swallows
                        beating up against the rafters,
        the architecture of consciousness
                        cracking.

It was how the fathers knew the past
        had trapdoors for falling in through sky,

            the children setting fire with their sandals
            to the stillness,
                        their clamor
                    pelting through the courtyard,
                disordering the epoch's endless nap.

Now the youngest comes to stand beside me
        lips slightly parted,
                her gaze following a swallow
                    lost inside the ceiling.

Sometimes it is hard to believe in anything

but the ocean grinding down below,
 dust settling along the window,
  wingtips softening the mission.

When I first wanted to fly,

 it was the blue translucence of the coast range
waiting like a mud room just before the afterworld,
  (the last dirt rinsed from soles,
   little jackets of gravity hanging on their pegs).

 It was the future kneeling beside my children
  at the spigot, lips pressed to rust,
water singing underground.

After Rain

Because the newness was green,
And the sky a clean, dark blue,

And the five bucks in the field
Ached with the world's goodness,

We crouched in the wet grass
To watch the albino stag

Trotting between the darker stars
Of his herd. There was his greater frailty,

And his shining, too—a kind of breakage
Trying the borders of beauty and want.

Beside us, under a Bishop pine,
The rain had coaxed amanitas

Into a drift of poison snow.
Brazen. Stupid. The bravado of loving

The burning skin
The spirit calls world—

The fallow deer carrying their majestic racks
Over the meadow's gold,

The sparrows
Spilling their slow leakage of being

Through the dead and living
Brush—and the brush

Already budded, already
Begging, *Ripen me, please—*

At Twelve Years

In the brief and sexless interval
of the fields,

she says, *I'm glad we die someday.*
All things need an end.

Her body lengthens.
The child in her melts

slowly, a winter swallow sent
North, a breathless changeling

climbing from the pool
where the boy in her

quietly drowns.
I know she feels it too:

the long time it takes
to become ourselves.

Oh, honey, the world can break
your heart with its forever,

while we go on leaving April.
Remember this unlatched gate

as a purity of being
        leading you back

to the whole country
        of beauty.

Remember the deer
        this morning, rising up

at first light, the rumpled grass
        she knelt down to scent,

exclaiming, *Look. Even the bodies of the deer*
        disappear in sleep.

Rain at Night

The child's silence wakes you.

And how long has she slept here,
her dream like milk cooling?

Now you stand at the window, shivering.
Rain grinds air into sugary phonemes.

Under the streetlight, inside the boundless halo
of light's crumby grain,
your neighbor bends stiffly, lifts his newspaper.

Three a.m., long past what is legible,

he wears his dead wife's sweater,
too tight to button, sleeves midway up his arms.

II.

I Tell Her About My Last Night With Her Father

There was an enormous river,
A rushing sound that filled the air with light.

I woke in late afternoon, alone.
He had left me

There, in the deepening secret of wilderness,
Calling out his name.

Of course, the river swallowed it all.

That afternoon I walked a clattering field of scree.
Came to a glacial lake, where I sat, thinking,

Original water. The place rain first touches down.

At dusk, the Wind Rivers turned gold, then red,
Before the steep gorge.

Before salvation and undoing
Appeared as the same fire,

And a four-point buck stepped into the icy lake,

And turned back.
Fastened his black eyes on mine

Until I saw one thing and knew another
About the dark we take together.

I undressed.
Gasped at the cold burning of the lake.

Swam toward the beautiful stillness
Of what, by nature, could not bear me near.

Awed at how close he'd let me come—

How long he'd waited
Before moving on.

Lake of Wings

i.

In the dream, the lake was more bird than water,
though we entered it,

though we parted the fluid whip
of wings, an endless rush of terns

breaking dark against our thighs,
a second sky

lashed around my neck. *Let me go,*
I begged, but you did not—

you held me tighter.

ii.

In the morning, rain picks itself up from the bay
and begins to fall again.

This is all the water there has ever been,
you say. Once I saw a milky vial

taken from a meteorite,
as if the vast and starry rooms of time

lived like that, in us:
the smallest sound you've ever heard

sweeping through the hour's evolution,
reckless slivers of the rain

vaulting through the largest distance
you could bear to know.

iii.

Each time I walk outside, a phoebe
flies out from her nest above the shed,

and from a willow, her liquid note,
her complaint.

Yes, I want to say to her, *it hurts,*
the youngest turning cartwheels

into the kitchen table, crying hard,
and then her sister staggering like a drunk

to dispute her sadness, so that climbing
from my lap, they leave together
laughing, out the door.

iv.

How quietly the children talk, in the backseat,
about the farmer's cows.

I've never touched one, the youngest says.

The herd thunders down the cliff.

Last night, our children built a tower
out of pillows and practiced falling,

shrieking as they jumped,

so that we could hear the terror of the flesh
that fastens us like sinew

to the occasions of our joy,

bats sipping from the spring, wind
singing out the erotic line of shore.

v.
They say each character in a dream
represents another aspect of the soul,

but when the lake of wings
I fought against

became a thousand birds
lifting me above the water,

I could feel the moorings swerve
and crack, the second chance

that is the slow explosion of the self,
a padlocked sky

pouring through my hair, my mouth,
the years like stars

hurtling backwards
through the luminous details,

the beautiful decoys.
And the part of me

I dream as you—
As what holds on

to the small violence of memory.
The light in its own time.

Argument for Transcendence with Child, Humming

This morning, the marsh glows in a sullen, preconscious light.
As if memorizing dissolution, she turns her head to sky,
long after a line of cormorants has grazed the bay.

And haven't I loved the almost gravity of her, all summer
in the musky light of the chicken coop, as she lifts the hens,
one by one, demanding, *Balance,* demanding *Fly.*

Beside me, her legs hurl skyward through a back walkover,
and the one body of the world follows after.
Exactly as the future dreamt it: an eventual darkness

fingering the ridge, the cove. And behind that, like a hallway
between tenses, the river dredging light
through cattails, rust-weed, sand.

The marsh snarls, cracks. She climbs into my lap,
as the chickens rustle in their coop.
Wind sighs and makes a clock of the willows,

the bramble heaving, as an elk crashes into the bay,
rack raised up. Stunned,
she looks out at the buck—dog-paddling, snorting—

then up at me.
How vulnerable, how impossibly heavy
we must seem, swimming across the narrow channel

of the visible world.
And the strange, tuneless current of her humming
that has not stopped, but goes on

carrying the elk
over the seabed, hooves not quite touching,
but lightened, changed,

before the next shore comes differently
together again, the fog burning back
the apparent cliffs, the ragged sky.

Vigil

Now the geese are crying for the falling year.

Adrift and on fire, flickers return from the blue hills.
Moths tear open the fierce green lawn,

like directions to the next world, tattered into bits,
shredded handfuls thrown up to sun.

Remember last Halloween, when our neighbor called
the animals and archangels, one by one, across his doorway,

and in they came, to his wife's hospital bed, frightened
but obedient, while he lifted their hands into hers.

Some things need to know they can still be touched.

Some things astonish us with the deeper names
of what was never meant to be

like the dream my child had of your guitar,

so certain that you'd brought the music back,
that she woke and padded down the hallway

to find me, here, alone, sewing her black cape and gown,
listening to the strange lantern of the geese

passing on . . .

And to My Answer, Which Is Yes, Which Is No

Once he knelt over me, begging to be touched.
Outside, wind rushed between the citrus trees,
the young fruit lashed and swaying,

and I felt how each tender gesture I refused
could never be given back
untouched, truly whole.

So that years later, when I finally drew him to me,
I knew that driven clean inside my desire,
was the scar of what would leave

even as it first arrived: his box of shirts
already laid inside the empty chest
of another woman's house,

our daughter stumbling after his disappearing car.

And yet tonight, there must be another,
more encompassing name for love,
planted as it is, inside these orchards

of pleasure and betrayal.
Because I'm sitting on the porch, listening
as our daughter tells me, on Wednesdays,

just before he drives her back across town,
how her father stops his finger-picking,
sets down his guitar, and begins, *a cappella,*

to croon the lovely particulars of her being.
Does it hurt you? she suddenly asks, her eyes
like his, so easily spilled with tears.

And yet, it's the kindness of her question
that roots me to the beauty of what was given,
no matter where it lives, or how.

And to my answer, which is yes, which is no.

Picking Wild Blackberries

After you ask my forgiveness,

I hang up the phone,
loop an empty can around my neck.

Wind wakes small sounds in the standing:
                birdhush,
                light scouring the hills,
                the unsayable wrongs.

Here, the utterly private ripens into pleasure,

and pleasure unfastens moths,
black flies, milkseed.

                And the pierce that punishes flesh
                even as it protects sweetness?

I stamp a crèche into bramble.

Pluck out a belled cluster with my left hand.
Pick with my right—
                each little ripeness
                thudding against tin.

Did I already say revelation is layered?

That the nethers are startled up—
An ache pulling the berries
                    down?

Because fidelity is not an order of magnitude,

and indifference not the only frontage road
running parallel to desire,

don't ask me about something I didn't do.

So what if there were a few stories:
the parachute he strapped to the dog
so she could float down from the roof,

or the job he had after college,
packing chutes for jumpers?

I don't have to tell you about the way he speaks:
the mathematical structure of his thought
built on the seduction of restraint,

his measured voice,
his hands resting on well-worn jeans. When you left me

briefly, to help your demented mother
wandering room to room,

don't forget you left your house torn open,
the children glazed with sweat,
air conditioner straining at the seams.

Don't forget this is July—
too hot to bike down beside the creek,

and the creek dried down to thistle,
the only water running underground.

So what if we took the kids to ice cream?

Sometimes you need to play at falling.
Sometimes, if you're lucky, you get near enough to ruin

to remember it all night long:
false moon of the porchlight
luring moths up against my hair, his lips, I swear

that never once touched mine.

Dark Carpenters

I'm not sure what the ants were waiting for—
the right heat or darkness,
a certain kind of silence turned up high.

But the night their wings broke through,

you cut your engine, the heat of your voice
leading me further down the dock.

Imagine stepping through a door into sea.

Imagine loving anything the way we do,
words poured onto the world's cold table,
and no language to name the shyness inside my desire.

A trawler shone its one light across the water's gun metal.
Above us, I remember long corridors of stars,

and closer in, bats lacing up the passageways of sky
as we turned and drove the coast highway south.

Did you take me there, only to see that door?

Did you want me to know we fall
and fall again,

into the black, black water of a life
we did not choose?

Or was it later, in that damp room,
a broken river of ants coursing through the walls,
your boots on the cement landing,
your hands on every door my body hid,

that you felt it too: all those wings unfurling,
love's dark carpenters
husking the absolute carapace of being,

breaking apart the old body
just to make it new?

Little Fever

Her frayed pajamas drag through grass. Unseasonably warm
In November, all the trees flushed and burning,

I hold her on the wooden deck, in sun.
We must invent it, each year, a little differently:

Her restless lengthening, this strange negotiation
Between mine and hers, want and letting go.

A few bees hover in the wild grape
Just before dying. She is nearly ten years old,

And there are only a few short days
Before winter begins in earnest.

Above us, a sudden handful of moths
Flare and glimmer, like exuberance torn from darkness.

We take this afternoon, this brief, unharnessed earth,
Lying in my arms.

Time As a Polygamist

Last night I dreamt I had to beg the first wife
for an hour alone with you. Tonight,

the stove is the second wife, the one
who snaps and hisses in a frantic heat.

Let's say history is a sanctuary
where the ghosts still have keys.

Let's say the floor trembles
with the din and grief of before.

The locks give—the flesh is portal.
Now the living enter, unspeakably hungry,

without memory, or the need of it.
Isn't this what the past was afraid of?

The new light we've shaved from limbs.
The necessary undoing, for now, undone.

My daughter tells me she is no longer a virgin,

just before Benicia on 680,
the Pacific glassy and wild in sun,

slow descent of the coastal mountains
gaining speed through the stunning green,

a flock of wrens
rushing to wake the dark between the trees.

Sure, there's plenty to be afraid of:
her future, spilling as it is carried forward.

How, already she knows
anyone can dream anyone into being,

his hand on the gorgeous swell of her thighs,
his hand anywhere he wants.

And there, above the freeway, a line of Holsteins
plodding home, udders swollen,

as if the entire horizon had ripened
into a sweetness asking to be let down.

There are tears in her eyes, in mine.
There are places no one ever expects to leave,

tiny nothing of her laid against my chest;
the everything that I was with her,

in those unmoored hours before dawn.

At the Heart

Today, leaving our daughter at college
there was a moment driving home

through the stalled and rusted vineyards,
when I wished I could have loved you better.

But later, listening to the geese in September,
the invisible filaments of their sad and lusty trumpets

calling through the vented holes of sky,
I swear I heard the days we turned from one another

as a worthy music played between the half-notes
of every day we turned back, amazed.

Sometimes I think love is unlearned knowledge,
and knowledge an unwillingness to throw away

too much, too fast. Sometimes I think violence
nestles at the heart of any life worth claiming.

Like the morning shoveling through the compost
when you uncovered a nest of rats, wincing

as you hurled your shovel down
on those pink and naked questions. Oh honey,

do you ever look up from thought
and sense the world before you came?

Or imagine the baby we gave back
as a gate falling backwards into beauty,

an extra angel posted at the awful intersection
of abundance. I don't think we were wrong.

And yet, sometimes I can't help but remember
a fierce afternoon in June, not long after,

when we'd climbed to the roof to pick
our first crop of twenty cherries—

sweetest in that year when the fruit came
long before we expected it—

when we knelt, shoulder to shoulder,
over our handful of tiny stones

and opened them, one by one, careful,
oh so careful, not to let a single drop

of that dark and gorgeous rain
spill through.

While she travels on, the small towns of each year flashing by,

her father trolls for halibut,
his reel dragging the tidal shine.

And even with the window open
and the bright green of cedar and fir
gilding the sky,

all I really want is to wake her from the future.

Now, her father returns empty-handed,
props his line behind the door.

Across the bay, the house on stilts is trembling.

Soon the shadows will throw off their overcoats,
which will float, all night, out to sea.

Soon the life I never stopped loving
will swarm
with its stars, its flaring memories

of her, at five, pinning and combing my hair,
asking if there was a before
only God remembers.

Perhaps I simply need to lie back
and the generous landscape will soften the edges.

Perhaps someone should remind me
loss is a train I boarded with her

so long ago, I almost forgot
that one day I would stand at a window

listening to the last cormorant
crying West—

a hoarse conductor calling out this destination
as mine.

Impossible Acres

Always the corn maize suggests a way out,
while the barn carries a river of children
deeper in.

A boy lifts a rabbit from the nesting box
and tucks it inside his shirt.

Always the light with its own ideas
about haysmoke, little knots of flies.

At dusk, the families drive home,
buckled into vans, cradling pumpkins,

the youngest child singing
to an entire world in need of comfort.

This close to the silence

the farmer's daughters sweep out stalls
before coming inside to watch T.V.

Even the crows have flown out
of the brittle stub
toward the lit and electric streets.

Silence Prepares Us for the Fields

That's what you said the day it was clear
we were no longer young,
the hillsides stunned with drifts of lupine.

Wild iris slit apart the meadow
with purple blades, and though damage
was a word I didn't want to use,

a hundred grebes dove at once:
a floating graveyard slipping underneath
the distant sea, and you beside me,

mumbling, *This is how the sky will look
when we are gone.* As if all that mattered
was that it did:

an endless rush of swallows
dragging shadows across the perfect quiet,
until there was nothing,

finally, but my hand
brushing slowly across your hair.
It was April. It was the argument

we had lost.
Not even touch to prepare us
finally, for the silence

of a body standing deep inside the fields,
listening to the little ivories of fescue
rising up, lying down, in wind.

On Whatever Form the Past Assumes Waiting for Us to Enter

Each evening, the pond draws in its breath of koi

and lets it out as stars and streetlights.
Memory pools in the yard's dark fjords,

while beyond us, tractors stand in fields
like sentries, waiting for deep night
to come alive.

The corn splits and shreds into silk.

My father calls from across the county
to catalogue the towns, the friends,
he is losing to the past.

A hunger not unlike hurt
gathers the fabled bodies, stony and patient

as statuary, as the delicate hands
that braid an hour into a life

here,
in the blackest halls of shrubbery,

all those mythic ears pricked to water,
the youngest child stepping outside before bed,

certain she has seen something

beneath the five cypresses, everything
suddenly poured into stillness, everything

listening.

III.

Girl with Watering Can, Speaks

—after Auguste Renoir's painting

Remember my blue dress buttoned up the front,
and the ribbon Monsieur insisted I wear,

burning like a cardinal on your bedroom wall.
I held my can as if just stopped,

though who could tell exactly
what I'd seen or heard. Still,

when I grew bored, there was the garden
around me, every leaf backlit by sun.

And the voices behind your door?
How you'd drop your grave smile

and become an artist's subject, too,
your body frozen in pose.

Remember how often you'd gaze at me
as if I were a window, a way out?

Or the afternoon you lifted me
off the wall? Turned me around

to touch the staples, wooden frame—
then hung me, quietly, back on the wall.

Back then, the unspoken was infinite
and tucked into everywhere.

Like the blossoming that came later,
the maples radiant and open

while I stood on my dirt path,
in the glare of orange-yellows

and gazed at the bloodred roses
that boy had brought you. And yes,

I should have been gladdened
that finally you became the window

I looked through, wondering
if perhaps the physical world was more

than a storehouse of light and symbol,
thinking, *This must be scent,*

and *this, desire:* His leather jacket
and your face buried in it.

His strange red hair
like so many stray threads of cadmium

brushed into your own dark blonde,
but changing, swept now

like morning's flush
across the bed's blue sky.

1964: A Litany

And the chicken pounded flat and flour-dusted
And turned six times in the spitting grease.
And her fat brown volumes of Julia Child
Laid open on the counter, pages stained with wine and milk.
Her housedress buttoned over Bermuda shorts.
The pan she'd bought in Mont St. Michel, brilliant copper,
Long, long handled, and the omelettes she folded once,
Kneeling at the basement hearth.
And the fondue pots and sterno cups and the clear, thin broth
With white, hairlike noodles and the finely chopped steak
And small, green onions.
The corn and beans snapped between her knees,
Her head turned up, staring out across the yard.
The wedge of iceberg lettuce,
Her body bristling in the kitchen,
And the oven's heated drawer where his dinner sat.
The cardinal she pointed to from the kitchen window
Before locking us outside to play.
And how he ate with us from time to time,
Rising more than once to knock my fork out of my hand.
And how that winter the sweet pears came in a box,
Wrapped in purple tissue, and she protested
They were for a party, and sulked,
While he laughed and cut them carefully,

His fingers dripping, slice by slice,
And fed us,
Our three mouths open, leaning out across the sink.

Star

Today we climbed the bluff
and lay along the edge of land.   Miles below,
water flung its lace across the blue.
        And I could hear the music of a spring
tipped from underneath these hills, something clear and perfect
loosening the storied levers of the earth.
        And then, further up the trail, a giant tire
thrown from a plane, and all around it
a wheel of iris sparking in the fields, as if a star had fallen
once and left its seeds, the way your mother, waking
just before she died, sang a lullaby you had never heard.
        No life ever leaves this earth, you told me then,
meaning, after death, we go on living
in someone else.

            Now, I want to ask if love
        goes on too, waiting out its turn,
the way a wildflower blooms first on land
that's been disturbed or torn,
        or the way this grass, alive with wind,
lay down all winter beneath the rain,
the passing shadows of the storms.
            And when we kneel down
inside the hillside's brief, amazing text
I can see that even here, inside each iris,
there is a flame:
        the stamens circled round in yellow,

and kindling sky to shore, a light so fierce
I wince,
        and whatever we call a soul
     so amazed to wake inside the damaged soil
of the flesh, it cannot help but ask,
    What finally hurt you into love?
    What star gave you the courage
      for such a stunning fall?

Summer

All night darkness ripens the hills.

All day, live oaks lean across the surface
raining glitter down

and the lake opens

as we enter, unclothed, buoyant,
our skin lit a phosphorescent green.

Ahead, a field of water lilies closes down.

A herd of elk watches from shore,
shaking their racks, side to side.

As if life had finally ruined us just enough
to be touched by everything doomed

but still alive, still answering
nothing—

how it calls,

how the susurrant oaks move
in the long arms of wind,

multiplying
the lake's patient glass,
their wanting audible.

In his last year,

my father stutters out to the porch and rests
against the rail, under occasional clouds.

Beyond us, blue hills and sparrows
carry the whole forgotten, the unearthed dream.

He believes the end is nothing
but the body's cochlea and passages, enfolded, silent.

He points to a fig tree snarled in a pine.
Tells me the gardener said to leave it alone, let it lean.

Time must be like a root on fire, a silent tongue
nosing through the moment's brush, the underside.

Strange what he's taught me about love—
How we are inflicted on each other.

How much comes from so little.
My hands are urgent as finches before winter,

that keep returning to his arm, his back—
to touch, to feed.

September under the Declining Zelkovas

The tree surgeon lays his enormous hand
against the emptied tree.

Leafless, leaden ache of sky. Quietly,

he sermonizes xylem, phloem,
termite-droppings and aphid-lace, months of rain and drought,
late-night swimmers, moths and owls creaking out at dusk,
our youngest climbing out too far, and the tumor

taking Pat so quickly, I had to beg the hospice nurse
to let me in. Even now,

wind quivers the living branches
that cross and touch across the street.

In the widening cistern of shadow, in the exhausting cul-de-sacs,
who among us refuses still to look?

And is it me
that asks, *Can we plant saplings beside the dying trees?*

The surgeon shakes his head.
Explains the young ones starve for light, shoot up
too fast and weaken, even as the old ones fall.

As God knows, sometimes it doesn't matter what you say or do.

Even in this generous hour, light thrown down
like rugs across the lawns.

She lived next door, and still I arrived too late—

Pat's finger tracing a scallop on the printed dress I wore,
her last words to me,

You should always look like summer.

Girl and Horse

She refuses chapter books, board games,
her mother's offer to drive her to the store.

Instead, she lies awake at noon,
studying the horses on her walls, stretching one hand out
to touch coarse mane, comic lips.

Sees herself leading the Quarter Horses out of storm.
Scents the feral, musky wet as she towels each mare dry.

Her mother calls her now to lunch.
Stupid chicken noodle soup, stupid milk, stupid yard and fences
someone dreamed up to keep the wild hampered.

Can't her mother hear them rustling down the hall?

Doesn't she know that horses can wait forever
for one undone gate?

That the moment you give up
is exactly where a horse will turn away and run?

This would be a good way to die,

he says, and swims out into the bay,
though I understand he's only thinking about his heart,

his death imminent and impossible
as the hard wind working against sky.

My daughter stands on shore, watching dusk redden
the far hills, asking, *Why is it more beautiful over there?*

What is clear to someone at the edge of a life?

Once I came down here alone, dragging my kayak behind,
astonished to see three otters rising like slender reeds
from the mouth of a vaster music,

and followed after,
through a wall of white fog, thinking, *The soul is a small vessel
paddling into the living fire of time.*

That morning has been working in me ever since

like threshold, like my old friend
trudging up the beach,

my daughter leaning against my chest,
a strand of her hair against my lips,
the hour like a window

out to where two kites collide and fall

into an endless aisle of waves going out,
coming back, one by one . . .

Laundry

We fold only to unfold again,
The unchosen, the next and next.

First the sheets, then the underthings.

Or the details of your dying: drop foot, fasciculations,
And then the weakness, palsy, paralysis.

How you drag yourself across the floor.

Tonight, I watch gusts of wind
Out the basement window, imagining you,

At twenty, beautifully muscled,
Your white shirt pressed, first two buttons open.

The dryer hums.
Stirs the momentary husks around and around.

I bend to my daughters' shirts, my husband's jeans.
Here, the outlines listen to my hands;

The matter conjured from a beloved margin

Holds,
Pressed to my chest, stays

Longer (how much longer?),
Stays

Warm.

Form as Equal Parts Punishment and Consolation

i.

Wind hectors the pines.
Breaks one branch into voice.

As if the too-long leaning
became a wren.

Became the dark syrup of sea
carrying the separate carapaces, the strenuous paddles,
across the hour's echo,

and in between the blue rustle of pines, the wild iris,

a widening cadenza of ruin,
its tender everywhere.

Incarnation,
or whatever it is we name
when we name the force of this world

passing into form, before passing on,

what happens to touch
when our hands have been swept away?

ii.

Underneath the late March clouds,
the oyster farmers shuck this morning's haul,
quick, dark minnows of their gloved hands
working the bubbled tanks,
knives tearing the ligneous hinges.

One worker cracks apart the shells.
Another hands us lime, red sauce.

What if incarnation cannot atone for silence?

What if we spread a blanket on the sand,
and the small girls—
the ones we carried across the water—

lie down between us,

so that clothed in hurt and pleasure,
we are more naked than the spirit will ever be?

iii.

Just across the road, the pauper's cemetery gleams.

Small wood crosses, plastic roses,
tiny windmill glinting silver.

If flesh is the language of desire,
and desire ages too,

then, before we sink into the entire gospel
of the unknown,

listen: A wheel of loons
rolls across the bay's trembling skin,

one half of the soul calling to the other,
The sky's a river,

and everywhere you look, you are breaking through.

Dead Pine

By the time the semi struck you, your flesh had already drunk
more dark than mine,

had already stumbled through
chorded halls of earth and stone.

Only the rafters of your leaves were left,
intaglios of the bones of sky

you had broken through, and this rock shelf
where a clean wind hammers saddles of the softest grey.

Soon the arborist will throw the ropes, tie the harness,
call your girth out

in a nimbus where you'll finally fall.
Like the patient who told me, as a child, he'd left his body

pinned beneath a school bus, while he rose above the cliffs
in a stalk of light. Once a week,

his gaze sliding along my shirt, he'd beg,
Tell me, what am I supposed to do?

with the years of vicodin, the jobs he couldn't keep,
debt collectors calling on a phone he wouldn't answer,

until I understood he wanted me
to take the body his life had ruined

and give it back, as it once had been—
prismatic, lustrous, whole.

Though he never said it. Though he wouldn't pay.
Though he drove one night through five cities

before passing out in his car, a vial of pills
spilled like yellow seeds around his shoes.

The day the coroner called,
I went to sit beside you and found a hive

drifting from your dying wood.
And the gold they carried, and the queen they robed,

swarming into a dark coil of hum—
well, it helped to think of him like that:

the spirit that he entered waiting like a robe

under the crushing weight
finally lifted from his spine,

so that the boy in the back seat—face pressed
against the rain-wet glass—

could finish what he started:

the road pitching suddenly
toward the blue-black hardness of the pines.

Before Rodin's "Gates of Hell"

Tomorrow is the first day of winter.
Recall, then, the long months of blossoming,

as if they were stories about the afterworld,
the burning just behind these bronze doors,

and sculpted there, Rodin's batlike creatures
splayed in fear, clinging to cornices,
grotesque with holding on.

You shuffle slowly around the museum's garden,
your tubing dragging us together.

Eden no longer seems the inverse of the underworld.

And this no longer seems your body,
but the small, inglorious swaddling around a soul.

And even if art defies the brevity of any singular life,

still there are the fields beyond these oaks,
wild with joy and rain.

And the tiny birds that fly out, shimmering

as we undress and clean you,
your weight suspended weakly between our arms.

We wrap your soiled clothes in grocery bags.
I want my life back, you say suddenly,

as the last light disappears, slips away.

Isn't this punishment enough?
What kind of God needs something more?

The Neighbor

When we first moved in, his wife was still alive,
and our youngest just a slip of flesh,

while the older two floated through the garden,
pretending to starve, shouting happily,
Sister, look what I've found now!

Meaning: we've been saved.

Meaning: there is a liturgy of near-misses
the soul hammers into a ladder
to climb back home.

Tonight, red lights wince along his lawn.
Paramedics needle lines, lock down a stretcher.

Death will always be a neighbor to someone,

and now, he lifts a hand in greeting
as they wheel him past.

A surprising softness
grazes my wrist, as he murmurs, *Hey, stranger.*

Meaning: *Nothing is as invisible as we'd like.*

Meaning: *I'm grateful how close you've come.*

At the Old Homestead in Cold Canyon

Equinox translates into balance.
A page slipped between two halves of dusk.

Once, in late sun, thousands of beetles
hung from grass,

and our daughter plucked a cluster, gently
cupped the strange red globe
in breath

until her handful fell away to wings.

Insects landed on the tumbled chimney,
the worn-down dirt, the paced-out stones.

But those that hovered in the roofless shade,
glittered like an alphabet shaken into sky.

Back before anyone learned to read,
the land held onto what happened.

The creek went on past belief.

At what point do we say
this is no longer a house?

Where the child left us?

Where she entered the known world?

Leaving the City

This morning, waking in a room twenty flights
above the street, we made love beneath a mirror.

Outside, willows, cypress, a flock of gulls
combing the span each falling thing endures.

So that now, going forward alone
through gold-brown hills, meadows fired into seed,

it seems something of you
rides with me into the brilliant wound of the world,

each field, each blade of fescue chiming
with the crossing, the unnamed hunger.

And here, where I pull off the highway
to wade into the swollen vines,

I feel gladness too,
for the thorns, for how it hurts—the brevity, the loneliness

of living in a single body, all the songs of a bearable size
pressing themselves against this meadow.

I wish you could see this too, how the thicket dust
appears to break and blossom—

like a wholeness finding out it was never whole,
but overfilled, spilling through the brush,

a cloud of pollen suspended above
the mule deers' startled going.

If there are ever times I want to leave you,
it is only because I believe we are already together

in the next world—
though I'm certain it looks just like this one:

a fiery pasture swept by seed,
the dark body of the forest turning around

whatever windfall of sudden matter enters:
the blossom, the berry, the buck and his two does

swaddled in the shadows' afterlight,
the willows' seamless door.

Maple Grace

        I walk as instructed,
just out of sight, while my daughter
trudges up the hill. Wind keeps on
smoothing winter's rain
deeper into the valley below us,
a dreamy ambling lifting up
the leafless stalks, my hair
strand by strand.
        And the lone Guernsey
up on the ridge, nervous,
shifting her weighty flanks
from hoof to hoof,
as my daughter approaches,
new grass laid in her palm.
        From where I stand,
I can't hear what sweetness,
what gentlings are offered,
but when she runs back into view,
the last child I will ever have
stops a few feet above me.
        This close, she says, excitedly,
before coming all the way down
to take my hand.
Still wanting the touch of my sameness.
Still the startling ignition of pleasure.
        Maple Grace, she says.
That's what I named her.

Hunger and a House Forever Sliding Out to Sea

i.

The children listen to the drumming standoff
of the rain and the answering quiet
the sea pours its arms around.
Is silence a sound? the eldest asks me.
And what if mercy were a house
forever sliding out to sea?
What if every asylum opened
in a field of songbirds?
What if you didn't yet know about POWs
and body counts and orphans
from Baghdad throwing themselves
onto the sidewalk, saying, *My mother,*
she looked like this, referring to the dead
staring absentmindedly up at sky?

ii.

In the morning my old friend helps me
clear the culverts. The wind seesaws,
pulls South, scatters tiny thistles of rain.
He tells me about the sadness
that started with a mouth cancer,
and now he cannot work, cannot sleep,
hears the birds as ghosts,
wants only to die.

We stand in the rich dark earth
threaded with leaves.
I try to push my hoe deeper in.
He lifts a shovelful of mud.
Is there anything that makes you happy? I ask.
Not even this, he says.
Not even talking to you.

iii.

After the betrayal and rage,
after the garden was abandoned and bolted,
some flew like the sharp bones of a prairie
         and some flew like the quail
in the rain-wet thistle, a thrumming
   that made the air more bass than drum.
And in the mind of the eldest oaks,
and in the trampled grass, and the vetch
beat askew, and in the handfuls of acorns
carried back, the newest animals
        did not know themselves
so much as they knew want and desire,
so much as all longing borrows form,
asking, *Who is there?*
        answering, *This is how a new country will come to be;*
        answering, *All you've ever lost.*

iv.

Would it be enough to remind him about hunger?
How it can return suddenly, without warning?
How loss resets the landscape of our illusions?

This morning I could not remember a rain
this beautiful or persistent. And hiking
with the children in their boots and hooded raincoats

and watching how easily
these girls moved through the glistening,
lifting ferns, touching blind hands under rocks,

slipping salamanders into a bucket, I did not understand
that, hours later, they would call me
to the back door, as one child tipped the bucket

and the other reached carefully in
to hurry those dark ponderers from one world
to another, humming with such pleasure

you'd think they were watching their own souls
stumbling into the creek—each awkward strider
become fluid, graceful, suddenly gone.

At Fourteen

Sometimes I want to touch her hair, her lips
and say, *Infinity is such a small word*

even as it leaks from the landscape
she ignores, refusing to follow my gaze

out across the shore.
There, along the water's surface,

a flock of cormorants ignites gold flurries.
And here I stand at the kitchen window,

listening to her shut and lock her door,
watching the hidden come forth

from the hidden, her childhood
already a lament deep inside me,

radiance dragging those birds
like a chain of gleaming links

across the sky's unruly floor.

Anorexia Nervosa

The Guest is inside you, and also inside me . . .

—Kabir

If we are all guests made of shining,
aching to feed one another on miracles,
then why is this girl in my office, slowly going dim?

And why, if the sea is a repository of light,
must we use the terrible ladder of one another
to climb out of the basement where she lives, unreached?

I don't know what I hate more: how every session
is the same—her dark eyes fevered, her hands
thin as water swept between floating ricks—

or how she once told me
I would miss her when she was gone.
Sometimes on my way home, I stop at Hog Island

to watch oyster farmers lean over their flatbottom boats,
sending down seed lines, hauling up giant buds of shell.
Sometimes the sea is a bright cauldron brimming with hunger,

and everyone shines beside the messenger's ladle.
Like the woman today, working the oyster counter;
How she pulled on her gloves, took up a knife.

On the house, she said to the man ahead of me,
And shucked a few sweetwaters,
before winking at the crowd drawn around her,

so rarely do we see appetite as the whole
salted wound, and then its quenching cup
of fire, given, in time.

My Father's Last Spring

Call it a season of iris drawn through straws,
paper whites smelling strangely of urine.
    Or call it a tree before fruit,
and point to small windows opening to bees.
    Then look further out,
at orchards exploding in cloud,
        ditch become ocean, become valley of gleam.
Call it lovely, uplifting, sublime,
        but please don't recite verses
on biblical clockwork, the time for each thing,
        explaining that this is an ordinary
mouthful of dirt exploding into freesias,
        the season when beauty's first breath sounds
drift into petals and literal gutters.
    And there's no need to remind me
that it never mattered which words I used.
    That he never listened,
back when he still could hear.
    But then, I've never told you
how once we held hands in a tiny backyard.
    Swing set, robin, telephone wire,
my father said slowly, after my first winter.
    Before I could talk, I thought it was all quiet
and soft and white without end.
    I wore a pink sweater and hat.
Out of experience, out of the cold,
        he took me to each sudden appearance,

each unspeakable story,
    and slowly, deliberately he called it
a world I could have.

Grunion Run

I wheel my father under a July moon,
past a night heron, the feral scent of public bathrooms.

When a terrier trots past,
he reaches out a hand to graze the prancing dog.

Soon the fish will leap onshore, lay their eggs,
return to sea, or die,

and there is a kind of courage in the undoing:
the subconscious cocked and ready,

my father's diminishment in my hands.
Below us, locals toss bottles into sand,

nurse fires in steel pits. Wait to dive
into the brief arena, hoping to catch a grunion

between their fingers—the small uncaught beings
jostled, touching—

whether it hurts or not,

whether you believe the dying

hang their gleaming attention just inside of,
or outside, time.

Elegy in Late August

This morning, the wind is all we have of time.
And though no one drowns, Tomales Bay seems an afterlife
our father would want to enter, the balloons lifting into sky

like little boats cornered in his breath,
and the body's torturous slowing
winding the joy of a dozen children taut.

Look at how they dive and leap
just beyond our reach.

Look at how their gravity dissolves
and then returns, as if to practice leaving.

I know you feel it too:
how the laurel bays nod to the horizon;

How the endpoints of our father's history
suspend us in the blue dream
of a late summer noon,
the children gathered now around the candles.

And as they bend to damp the flame,
I want you to put your arm in mine;
I want to touch the girls we once were,
in exactly the way they need,
I want them to hear you whispering, *It will be alright,*

just as here, high above the bay,
cormorants arrow west.

Their wings make a thrumming cloak
as they rush past, and then just as quickly
fall away,

so that suddenly we are undressed
of our shame, and perilously beautiful

in the winter of what follows after:
that orchard of dark
unfolding in the distance—   always the distance

ripening, gathering weight.

Tomales Bay

We lie down on the dock
and listen to wind fingering the masts,

a kind of chiming you say
that always makes you sad.

A gull slips through the bay,
lifting white and impossible into sky.

And there, just beyond the cove,
a man and his two small boys

shout wildly, clapping at each mackerel
they drag up over their rowboat's stern.

The water's surface keeps breaking.
The sky keeps changing colors.

And behind it, behind beauty?

Perhaps we were not meant
to understand everything.

Perhaps it doesn't matter
how far away the disturbance
travels to reach us,

or how hard the slam and thrust
buried in these waves.

Our bodies are sleeved in light.

And our souls,
they make this trip alone.

Happiness

When light shaves obsidian into shine
and shore gapes mouthfuls of dark winter sand

and water talks the way a dog talks
with his whole body leaping into air

and the spray, still warm, gathers into swallows
zipping close enough to electrify the wind

around your lips and it tastes of salt
and white tulips opening into furrows

of wave and wingblades—numberless seabirds
scared up, so that the plow of their rising

uncovers a bull seal peering out at your kayak,
eager as the child you carry across the bay

and quietly over the cold linger, she is
singing, then you are, yes, this is

Night Light

Your rhythmic stroke peels back
an edge of undertow, delicate as lace.

Behind you, seals dive, thumping your kayak
in a late afternoon so quiet

the essential hazards of shape
are healing themselves into mist.   Oh, deep swimmers

knocking against the door of what you always believed,
there are portals everywhere:

you only have to stay dumb and alive
to what speaks in so many fallible, complicated tongues;

you only have to brave the terror of one being
beseeching the other.

Now a flock of cormorants
wheels up from shore, heading west.

Now the dying write letters across the sky,
asking, *What gate did you pass through*

to reach this darkening?
And the choir of white stars,

chiming silently, briefly—
a blizzard of moon jellies floating past—

if you carry anything now, let it be the seals
rising up to watch you glide away.

Let the orb glowing above it all
remind you, that somewhere

between eternity and evening,
the world once left a light on . . .

Notes

The epigraph from *Demetrecopolou Wintun Songs*, edited by Robert Fleming Heizer and Albert B. Elasser, is quoted in Mike Madison's *Walking the Flatlands: The Rural Landscape of the Lower Sacramento Valley* (Berkeley, California: Heyday Books, 2002), page 25.

"Driving West on 37, Listening to the Sonic Memorial"—The Sonic Memorial is a collaborative project of all recordings, voicemails, etc., from the victims of 9/11 and their loved ones.

"Proof, As Near As I Can Tell"—for L.C.

"Gristled Angels"— for V.

"Flyway"—The fragment, "layers of giving up," is stolen from Brenda Hillman's poem, "Franciscan Complex" in *Cascadia*.

"Eighteen Days," "Heaven," "Girl and Horse," "Argument for Transcendence," "Little Fever," "Maple Grace," "Happiness"—for Mia.

"Golden Gate," "At Twelve Years," "At the Old Homestead," "At Fourteen"—for Hannah.

"Easter Sunday," "I Tell Her About My Last Night," "Vigil," "My daughter tells me," "While she travels on," "Tomales Bay"—for Sophie.

"Rain at Night," "The Neighbor"— in memory of Noel Patton.

"Lake of Wings," "Anniversary," "At the Heart," "Dark Carpenters Leaving the City"—for Steve.

"And to my answer which is yes, which is no"—for Sophie, after a poem by Ruth Schwartz.

"Star"—for Joanne, after a poem by Robin Behn.

"September under the Declining Zelkova"—in memory of Patricia Patton.

"Dead Pine"—in memory of D.P.

"Before Rodin's Gates of Hell"—for Miriam Stombler.

"This would be a good way to die," "Hunger and a House Forever Sliding Out to Sea"— for Bennett.

"Elegy in Late August"—the original version of this poem was written in memory of Pat Rizzo, for Ellen Cohen.

"Night Light"— in memory of Lily Cohen.

Acknowledgments

Thanks to the editors of the following journals, in which these poems first appeared, in slightly different versions, and/or with different titles: *Crab Orchard Review*: "1964: A Litany"; *descant*: "After Rain," "Dark Carpenters"; *The Grist*: "And to My Answer, Which Is Yes, Which Is No"; *Parthenon West Review*: "Heaven," "Vigil," "Leaving the City," "Argument for Transcendence with Child, Humming," "Elegy in Late August"; *Poetry Now*: "Dead Pines," "Gristled Angels," "On Whatever Form the Past Assumes Waiting for Us to Enter"; *The Pinch*: "At Heart."

"Heaven," was chosen by the San Francisco Center for the Book to be printed as a broadside in a limited edition.

I also wish to thank Gemini Ink and the Napa Valley Writers' Conference for partial fellowships to attend their programs, during which some of these poems were completed.

I'd also like to thank Jeff Gundy, Katherine Northrop, Ruth Schwartz for their invaluable friendship and insightful editorial suggestions. Lisa Abraham, Cyrus Cassells, Cathy French, Brigit Pegeen Kelly, and Denise Lichtig also helped with revisions on many of these poems. And, of course, thank you to my family, who graciously offer me time and space, but most importantly, love. And finally, thanks to my father for his courage, integrity, and deep love for this world.

About the Author

Julia Levine's poetry collections include *Ask*—winner of the 2002 Tampa Review Prize for Poetry—and *Practicing for Heaven*, which won the 1998 Anhinga Prize for Poetry, as well as a bronze medal from *ForeWord* magazine. She has received numerous awards and grants in poetry, including the Discovery/*The Nation* Award for Emerging New Writers, the Pablo Neruda Prize in poetry, a California State Arts Council Grant, as well as five Pushcart Prize nominations. Her poems have been published in many journals, including *Ploughshares*, *The Nation*, *Southern Poetry Review*, *Prairie Schooner*, and *Crab Orchard Poetry Review*. She received her Ph.D. from University of California at Berkeley in clinical psychology. She lives and works in Davis, California.

About the Book

Ditch-tender is set in Adobe Garamond Pro types based on the sixteenth century roman types of Claude Garamond and the complementary italic types of Robert Granjon. The title is set in Michelangelo, a script font adapted from the handwriting of the famous artist and created in association with the Philadelphia Museum of Art by P22 Type Foundry of Buffalo, New York. The book was designed and typeset by Richard Mathews at the University of Tampa Press.

POETRY FROM THE UNIVERSITY OF TAMPA PRESS

* Denotes winner of the Tampa Review Prize for Poetry